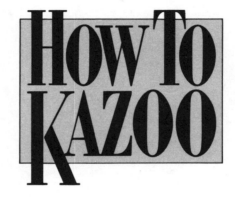

How To Kazoo

BARBARA STEWART

Photographs by
JERRY DARVIN

Illustrations by
PHILIP A. SCHEUER

WORKMAN
PUBLISHING
NEW YORK

Library of Congress Cataloging in Publication Data
Stewart, Barbara.
  How to kazoo.
  Discography: p. 91
  1. Kazoo—Methods—Self-instruction. I. Title.
MT533.K36S73 1983   788'.5   83-40032
ISBN 0-89480-605-X

Cover and book design: Douglass Grimmett
Cover and book photographs: Jerry Darvin
Illustrations: Philip A. Scheuer

Workman Publishing Company, Inc.
708 Broadway
New York, NY 10003

Manufactured in the United States of America
First printing October 1983
20 19 18 17 16 15 14

Dedication

To kazoodaphiles everywhere

John Stanton

Acknowledgments

I gratefully acknowledge the enthusiastic assistance of kazoodaphiles everywhere, especially the following: expert kazooists Allison and Whitney Stewart (my daughters); my mom (not-so-expert kazooist, but a great help nevertheless); Dr. Andrew Dean; my editor Suzanne Rafer (a staunch defender of kazoodaism); Barry Marx; Jerry Darvin; Rowena McDade; Jim Harrison; Gideon Schein; Jerry Edelstein; Kazoophony members Lance Lehmberg, Chuck Morey, Bill Dengler, Alan Bunin, Mark Wolf, and Kim Scharnberg; Vince, Jane, and Alicia McConnell; Mary Speers; Susan Balsam; Randy Hoey; Ginny

Hoyt; Harry Smith; Carol Crow; Stefan Lundbach; Dena Epstein; Alan Lomax; Michael Watson (Jr. and Sr.); Simon Pontin; Joyce Hangartner; Ross and Janie Reynolds; Professor Roger Remington; Bill Sabia; Mel Simon; Robert Cavala; Ray Joseph; Edith Efron (a real writer); Mary Anne Sterling; John Menihan, Jr.; Ruth and Bill Cahn; Margie Lu and Professor David Perlman; Hank and Ann Couch; John Stanton; Tim Kelley; Dave Frank; Silas Pendelton III; Bill Snyder; Sally Schenk; Mimi and John Thomas; Taft and Masako Toribara; Rep. Frank Horton; Paul Newman; Sandy Lehmberg and the Kazoophony Supply Depot; Kazooperman (Rob Spoor); John Marcellus; the Hohner Company; the Kazoo Company, Inc.; Trophy Music, Inc.; Dr. David Evans (Memphis State University); Dr. Samuel Floyd, Jr.; Country Music Museum (Nashville); Robert Sheldon and Mike Licht (Smithsonian Institution); University of Indiana Music Library; Ruth Watanabe and Ross Wood (Eastman School of Music Library); Ronald Searle; John and Nonnie Locke; John Goldberg and Greg Mott; Sir Arthur Shafman (Ludakravian Ambassador, friend, and manager); and Sir Eric Ashworth, faithful literary agent.

Thanks also to models Doug Grimmett; Julienne McNeer; Beverly McClain; Jennifer Rogers; Thomas Hill; Paul Hanson; Wayne Kirn; Erica Gjersvik; Sallie Jackson; Maureen Kelly; and Bert Snyder.

Finally, I am grateful to IBM, whose 418 feet of lift-off erasure tapes for my typewriter deleted an estimated 8,800 words, making the book of workable size for publication.

> **"If nobody wants to go to your concert, nothing will stop them."** —Isaac Stern

Contents

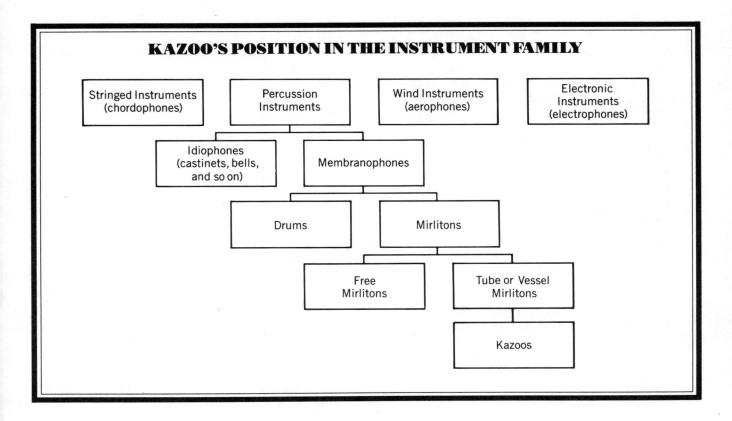

KAZOO'S POSITION IN THE INSTRUMENT FAMILY

Stringed Instruments (chordophones)

Percussion Instruments

Wind Instruments (aerophones)

Electronic Instruments (electrophones)

Idiophones (castinets, bells, and so on)

Membranophones

Drums

Mirlitons

Free Mirlitons

Tube or Vessel Mirlitons

Kazoos

Kazoo (kə-zōō′) n. 1. A manufactured version of an Afro-American folk instrument, U.S. in origin. An auxiliary instrument of the membranophone category, a specific type of tube mirliton, in which sound is vocally produced by humming, singing, or speaking into the larger end of an open-ended, cigar-shaped tube. A stretched membrane in the top of the instrument is set in vibration by the air column and modifies the sound into a nasal buzzing timbre. The tube is usually made of metal (tin, sometimes gold-plated) or plastic, with a removable turret on top that unscrews or lifts out to allow replacement of the membrane. The resonating membrane is of animal membrane, plastic or wax paper. The kazoo is closely related to but not identical to the abeng, akasitori, bazoo, Bigotphone (Bigophone), cantophone, chalumeau eunuque, Düderli, eggwara, eunuch flute, faggotzug, fipple flute, Flatsche, flauto di voce, free mirliton (comb and tissue paper), French mirliton, hewgag, Hum-a-zoo®, konene, mbanakum, megablaster, merlotina, nyastaranga, onion flute, shalmei, Skalmej, Strählorgelj, sudrophone, turkey caller, varinette, vocaphone, zazah, and zobo.

free mirlitons (such as the comb and tissue paper or the turkey call) or *tube* or *vessel mirlitons* (such as the zobo, kazoo, and eunuch flute).

Just as more conventional instruments have specific names, so do the types of tube mirlitons. Violin, for example, is a specific name for a particular shape and type of chordophone, subcategory lute. No sensible person would refer to a violin as a "lute," although it does belong to this group of instruments. Nor would we use violin as a synonym for the hurdy-gurdy or bass viol, even though they are related in principles of sound production. In like fashion, we correctly use "kazoo" to refer to a specific instrument, the American version of a tube mirliton.

An African Heritage

What a culture considers sacred is often obscured in veils of secrecy that conceal its true purpose. Such is the case with the African mirlitons, forerunners of American kazoos. While it is known they were used in sacred ceremonies, the exact purpose of the instrument has remained largely a mystery to the outside world.

Most musicologists and anthropologists have assumed they were used for producing musical sounds but this is not so. The African mirlitons were primarily used as voice disguisers and as weapons of intimidation, not instruments.

Mirlitons appeared in a surprising number of cultures throughout Africa. They varied considerably in size and shape from tribe to tribe, yet a style found in many cultures is a hollow tube, covered at each end by a membrane, with a center mouthpiece. Tubes are made of an endless variety of materials, including: bones, reeds, gourds, corn stalks, buffalo horns, and even human skulls.

The instrument was used to impersonate the voices of the dead, to make terrifying sounds and bring messages from the spirit world. The male ceremonial figure concealed his true identity by enshrouding himself in robes (and often a mask) and by using a mirliton to disguise his voice. The messages from the "spirits of the dead" were communicated in this manner and the distorted sounds were often interpreted by tribal officials to be sure the meaning was clear.

The effectiveness of the intimidation depended on preserving the secret of the existence of voice disguisers (mirlitons), since once the source was revealed, the fear of the unknown would no longer be a factor. For this reason, to reveal the secret to an outsider, or to a woman or uninitiated male tribe member, was an offense punishable by death.

REASONS FOR KAZOOING

Kazooists are often asked the question, "Why do you kazoo?" There is no need to dignify such a question with a lengthy reply. Instead a well-chosen short retort will rid you of the questioner and allow you to get to your serious practicing.

I kazoo because:

1. It's there.
2. It requires no prior experience.
3. It's a wonderful leveler, making the finest singers sound no better or worse than I do.
4. It may be that it's none of your business, Bub.
5. The harmonica class was full.
6. At the time, it seemed like the thing to do.
7. I bought one by mistake and the store wouldn't take it back.
8. I got a hernia from carrying my piano around.
9. I can't help myself, the devil makes me do it.
10. It's fun.
11. Everyone should be an expert at something and this field is wide open.

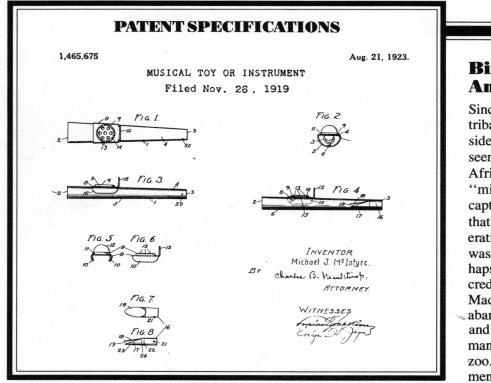

PATENT SPECIFICATIONS

1,465,675

Aug. 21, 1923.

MUSICAL TOY OR INSTRUMENT
Filed Nov. 26, 1919

FIG. 1.

FIG. 2.

FIG. 3.

FIG. 4.

FIG. 5. FIG. 6.

FIG. 7.

FIG. 8.

INVENTOR
Michael J. McIntyre.

BY Charles B. Hamltrop.
ATTORNEY.

WITNESSES

Birth of the Kazoo in America

Since divulging the secret of the tribal "voice disguiser" to an outsider was punishable by death, it seems very unlikely that any of the African slaves would have held "mirliton show and tell" for their captors. However, it *is* plausible that an American descendant, generations removed from tribal ritual, was familiar with the mirliton, perhaps even without knowing its sacred function. Legend has it that in Macon, Georgia, in the 1840s, Alabama Vest, an American black, and Thaddeus Von Clegg, a German clockmaker, invented the kazoo. Von Clegg made the instrument to Vest's specifications. It was reported to have been exhibited at the Georgia State Fair in 1852 before being sold to a toy manufacturer, who produced it under the name "Down South Submarine."*

Although I have not found other reports to substantiate this particular account, both the *Oxford English Dictionary* and *Grove's Dictionary of Music and Musicians* agree that the kazoo is American. And if we can't believe *Grove's Dictionary* and the *Oxford English Dictionary,* who *can* we trust?

Whatever its exact origins, the submarine-shaped kazoo was an acoustic improvement on the more primitive mirlitons because the tur-

ret on the top (not seen in African mirlitons) acted as a collector for exterior vibrations. The turret's screw-on flange allowed easy replacement of damaged or worn membranes.

The kazoo took on an important role as a musical instrument in blues and country music in the United States. From the 1850s on, musicians used kazoos to amplify their voices, to make them loud enough to compete with stringed instruments. The kazoo made an easy transition to jazz. Along with the comb and tissue paper, it would appear throughout jazz history. It was inexpensive and readily available, and in the hands of an expert, phenomenal effects could be achieved.

*Green, Parp, *Melody Maker and Rhythm,* October 20, 1951, page 11.

United Press International

Albert Einstein was known to have played the violin, the musical spoons, and the kazoo, not necessarily simultaneously.

Although it is no longer a weapon, some critics argue there is still an element of intimidation remaining. Particularly convincing on this point are school bus drivers who have been intimidated by exuberant kazoo-wielding children.

Where Kazoos Come From

Most kazoos today are produced by three major companies:

The Hohner Company of Richmond, Va., well known for its harmonicas, is now producing an excellent standard plastic kazoo which gives surprisingly good tone quality, and has the advantage of being noncorrosive.

The Kazoo Company of Eden, N.Y., is the only manufacturer (since 1902) of the metal kazoo. At the present time, it is the world's largest kazoo manufacturer. The construction of their kazoos is well engineered for musicality and is suitable for the serious kazooist.

The Kazoo Company manufactures several kinds of metal kazoos, using the same principles of acoustical sound production (tubular body, with resonator placed at top). They vary in size and decorative features and resemble traditional band instruments. Purists, of course, prefer the unadulterated bombardment of sound produced by the standard submarine-shaped model.

The third major kazoo manufacturer is **Trophy Music** of Cleveland, Ohio. They manufacture the Hum-a-Zoo® and also distribute the more traditional submarine-shaped kazoos.

Kazoophony Supply Depot is a distributor of kazoos. They are located at 3316 Chalet Court, Sioux City, Iowa 51106.

Home of the Kazoo Company.

Keep America Humming

If you can hum, sing, or talk, you can successfully kazoo. At this very moment, millions of satisfied kazooists all over the globe are delighting in its distinctive sounds. Yet sadly, the kazoo continues to be an object of derision and scorn among those ignorant of its extraordinary qualities. The time has come to set the record straight and allow the kazoo to take its rightful place in the world of music.

For the uninitiated, the kazoo is a small cigar-shaped plastic or metal instrument that produces a pleasant buzzing when the player hums, sings, or speaks into it. The instrument itself has no musical capabilities, so everything depends on the kazooist. In fact, it has been said that the instrument may actually be a hindrance to the kazooist, that "the kazoo is to music what the full body cast is to ballet." But this is a very shortsighted view. The kazoo's total dependency on the creative capabilities of the kazooist is precisely what makes kazooing a uniquely individual musical expression.

Importantly, the kazoo *is* a musical instrument, not simply a toy. Thus, for all kazooists, the fundamental rule of musicianship applies: "Practice, practice, practice . . . but not near the neighbors."

The Kazoo and Its Place in the Musicological Hierarchy

Although musicologists are great experts on many things, the kazoo is not one of them. Preoccupied with other matters, musicologists have tended to classify anything that buzzes as a kazoo. The kazoo, eunuch flute, mirliton, Hum-a-zoo®, zobo, and other similar instruments have all been wantonly and erroneously thrown together and used interchangeably. Some have even gone so far afield as to confuse the kazoo with the ocarina (sweet potato) and such items as the Jew's harp, harmonica, or the whoopee cushion. (Fortunately, most of these experts remain cloistered in academia and do not frequent the out-of-doors. Otherwise, the confusion might extend to include chain saws, model airplanes, and even killer bees.)

The kazoo is actually a member of the musical classification

"membranophone." This category consists of percussion instruments wherein sound is produced through use of a stretched membrane. Further, it is part of the subcategory, "mirlitons," a group of instruments that disguises or modifies sounds produced vocally (or by another instrument) through the medium of vibrating membranes. The membrane causes the sound to be amplified and distorted, giving a nasal buzzing quality.

There are a thousand varieties of mirlitons throughout the world. They share the same principle of sound production but exist in varying sizes, shapes, and permutations in different countries. This vastly popular group of instruments may be further subcategorized as either

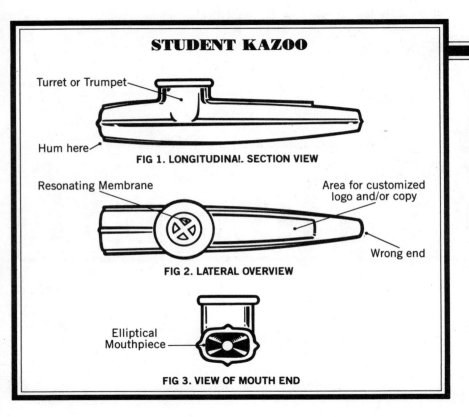

STUDENT KAZOO

Turret or Trumpet

Hum here

FIG 1. LONGITUDINAL SECTION VIEW

Resonating Membrane

Area for customized logo and/or copy

Wrong end

FIG 2. LATERAL OVERVIEW

Elliptical Mouthpiece

FIG 3. VIEW OF MOUTH END

Choosing an Instrument

For those who bought this book, the choice has already been made. But, sooner or later you may need or wish to purchase a new kazoo.

Your Student Model

The kazoo you received with this manual is the professional student model made of Pro-Fax® polypropylene copolymer flake and premix. It is manufactured by the Hohner Company. It has a:

- Specific gravity of 0.88–0.92

- Melting point of 160°C (320°F)

- Flash point of 329°C or 625°F (Setchkin)

- Autoignition temperature of 357°C or 675°F (Setchkin)
- Molecular weight greater than 200,000 (without membrane).

King Kazoo (metal)

The basic metal kazoo (page 22) is submarine or cigar-shaped, in the tradition of the original "Down South Submarine." It is constructed of sheet metal (tin) and painted with non-toxic paint.

At the top is a turret containing the resonating membrane (reed). The resonating membrane is also called a vibrator or diaphragm, but usually is referred to by professional kazooists as "the little paper thing on the top." It is made of animal membrane, plastic, or wax paper and is held in place in the turret by a screwed flange (the spadger).

Metal kazoos are manufactured by a metal stamping procedure. The halves are punched from lithographed sheets of tin-plated steel, which are between 0.008-0.012 of an inch thick (the same material used for tin cans). The halves are then shaped with presses and rolled in quantity. The diaphragms are stamped and mounted on separate machines. The placement of the membrane inside the turret and the turret assembly (screwing in the flange) is done manually by kazoo assembly workers.

OCCUPATIONAL HAZARD

Tendonitis of the wrist is a known occupational hazard of those who work in kazoo factories. It occurs among the turret assembly line workers who spend extensive time twisting tops. This orthopedic problem is also common among badminton and squash players and "sheet shakers" (workers who fluff out and fold sheets) in laundries.

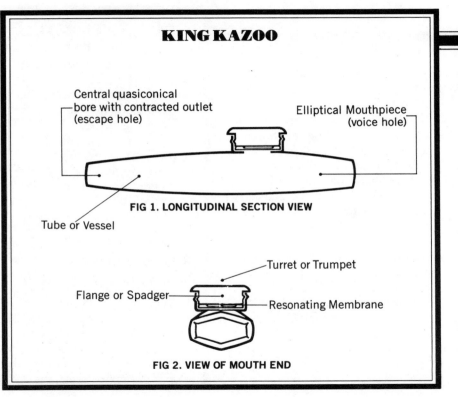

KING KAZOO

Central quasiconical
bore with contracted outlet
(escape hole)

Elliptical Mouthpiece
(voice hole)

FIG 1. LONGITUDINAL SECTION VIEW

Tube or Vessel

Turret or Trumpet

Flange or Spadger

Resonating Membrane

FIG 2. VIEW OF MOUTH END

Resonating Membranes

Until recently, the resonating membrane used in metal kazoos was made exclusively of animal membrane, stretched and held in place by a tiny circular frame of cardboard. This membrane, extracted from sheep or cow stomachs (without their consent), is the same material used to cap perfume bottles, since it is impervious to the scent and resists water and solvents.

Rising sheep prices in Australia and competition from dog food companies created a dramatic increase in the price of the membrane, causing the Kazoo Company, Inc., to go to a plastic (silicon) resonator. This new reso-

·nator is more durable and less susceptible to breakage, but gives a slightly sharper and less pleasant tone color.

The resonating membrane in

Beware of membrane disintegration.

most plastic kazoos is made of wax paper. The wax paper resonators are simply cut in a round shape to fit, without requiring a cardboard frame to stretch or anchor it. Contrary to folklore, tissue paper and, even worse, non-European toilet paper, are unacceptable, since they lack sharp resolution or resonance. They also disintegrate when repeatedly exposed to moisture.

Acoustical Properties of Kazoo Sound

The column of sound waves, supplied by the vocalization of the kazooist, travels into the barrel of the kazoo through the elliptical mouthhole. When the sound waves strike the resonating membrane, they are magnified and distorted.

In the interior of the barrel or resonating chamber, these vibrations are propelled in all directions, resonating from the membrane and meeting new vibrations as they are set in motion. The sounds escape through the anterior (opposite end from the mouthpiece) and also from the turret. The effect is a series of complicated layers of overtones, which the listener hears as a buzzing timbre (fuzzy pitch).

Exterior vibrations (outer-air vibrations) are emitted from the top of the resonating membrane. Some of these escape into the external air and some are entrapped in the turret or trumpet of the instrument, causing them to interact with the new sets of vibrations.

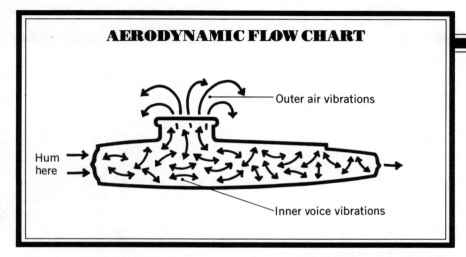

AERODYNAMIC FLOW CHART

Outer air vibrations

Hum here

Inner voice vibrations

The best kazoo sounds occur at the turret outlet. This is because these vibrations are more dense and less airy sounding than the weaker inner voice vibrations that must travel long distances and have less interaction with the membrane.

In the case of stringed instruments, *sympathetic vibrations* occur when a string is set in motion in response to vibrations of the same pitch from another source. For example, a "ghost effect" can be achieved while standing next to a piano and playing a pitch on the violin. The piano string of the same pitch frequency will begin to spontaneously vibrate, causing the eerie "ghost effect." Sympathetic vibration responds only to vibrations of the same pitch.

On the other hand, the principle of kazoo sound production is what we shall term *antagonistic vibration*. The resonating membrane, rather than being sympathetic to a particular pitch is nondiscriminating, capable of being set in motion by nearly anything. The sound from the voice, which sets the membrane in vibration, is rebounded in all directions from the membrane, setting up a conflict with any new vibrations being created by the player. This results in a bombardment of sound and produces the fuzzy nasal timbre so highly valued by the kazooist.

Care and Maintenance of the Kazoo

The kazoo should be cleaned as needed, since such things as dirt, spittle, dust, insects, and tar spots adhere firmly to the body and may damage the paintwork. (They also taste terrible.) Pipe cleaners or cotton swabs can be used to clear the tube of foreign matter. During the winter, special care should be taken to wash off all road salt residue as soon as possible to prevent corrosion of the metal kazoo.

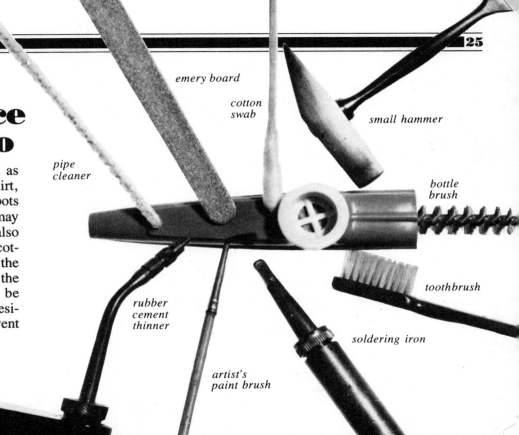

emery board

cotton swab

small hammer

pipe cleaner

bottle brush

toothbrush

rubber cement thinner

soldering iron

artist's paint brush

Washing (plastic or metal models)

When washing the kazoo, do not expose it to direct sunlight. For the plastic models, simply wipe the outer surfaces with a damp sponge or soft cloth. If the membrane is not removable, do not submerge the kazoo in water.

For the metal models, remove the membrane from the turret and set aside. Soften up the dirt on the inside of the kazoo with a water jet and then rinse the whole body with a light jet until the dirt has loos-

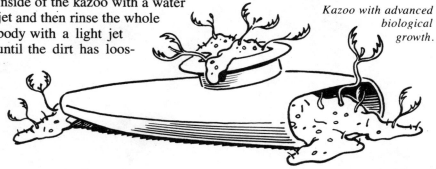

ened. Wash off the dirt with a tiny sponge, using plenty of lukewarm, *not* hot, water. Then dry carefully with a soft clean cloth. Replace the membrane in the turret.

Note: Asphalt spots, tar pittings, and gum wads can be removed with kerosene or tar removers, but this may leave a bitter aftertaste, besides possibly being toxic. For this reason, kazooists experiencing

Kazoo with advanced biological growth.

severe maintenance problems of this nature are advised to discard the instrument and buy a new one.

In humid climates watch for biological growth or base side scum in the interior channel of the tube. A clear solution of household cleanser with ammonia will alleviate the biological growth problem, but may be injurious to the player. In this case, it is also best to discard the offending instrument and replace it with a new, uncontaminated one.

Anti-Rust Treatment
(metal kazoos only)

Your kazoo may have been anti-rust treated at its factory inspection. If so, only a touch-up of the anti-rust treatment need be done. If touching-up is necessary, this should be done immediately to prevent moisture from seeping in and consequently causing damage. While working on the body, remember to remove the membrane to prevent moisture damage.

Polishing (metal kazoos only)

The kazoo does not need polishing unless the surface finish begins to lose its luster and normal washing is no longer sufficient to make it shine again. Under normal conditions, it is sufficient to polish the kazoo once or twice a year, assuming that it is cared for and washed as soon as it becomes dirty or clogged. Before the kazoo is polished, it should be carefully washed and dried to avoid

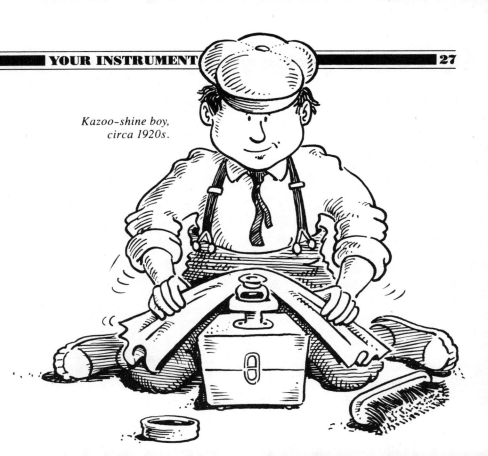

Kazoo-shine boy, circa 1920s.

scratches on the paintwork.

Use household paraffin (the same wax that is used to seal home-canned foods) or mustache wax to polish your kazoo.

Before applying be sure the surface is absolutely clean. Waxing should neither be considered a substitute for polishing nor a necessary protection for the paintwork against unfavorable weather. For the most part, waxing is not necessary until at least a year following delivery of the kazoo.

Body Work (metal kazoos only)

To prevent the kazoo from sustaining dent damage, it is important as a preventive measure to caution all kazooists to watch where they step. Care should also be exercised to avoid dropping the instrument. If damaged, standard body work techniques may be used to hammer out dents. Touch-up procedures should then be followed.

Paint Touch-up
(metal kazoos only)

Paint damage requires immediate attention to avoid rusting. Make it a habit to check the finish regularly and touch-up if necessary, particularly in the mouthpiece area.

Minor scratches and chips can be repaired by using non-toxic primer and paint. For deep scars:

1. Scrape or sand the damaged surface lightly to break the edges of the scar.

2. Thoroughly mix the primer and apply it with a small brush, toothpick or matchstick.

3. When the primed surface is dry, the paint can be applied by brush. Mix paint thoroughly, apply several thin paint coats and dry after each application.

4. If your kazoo is two-colored, you may want to mask the center area to protect surrounding paint.

Use of Bore Oil
(metal kazoos)

Instrumentalists often ask whether they should use bore oil on the kazoo to prevent sticking of the movable parts. I personally use it sparingly and only when the instrument is severely infested with bores.

Resonator Check
(plastic and metal kazoos)

At regular intervals, the resonating membrane should be checked for irregularities or breaks. A hole in the membrane indicates an emergency situation, requiring immediate replacement.

For plastic models with nonremovable membranes it means the purchase of an entirely new instrument.

*Close up
of resonator hole.*

Care and Maintenance of the Kazooist

Lip Fatigue

Lip fatigue may be prevented by pacing yourself. Have short practice time periods, gradually lengthening the sessions as you strengthen your embouchure muscles (see page 33) and build your endurance threshhold.

Chapping, Chafing, and Blistering

Lip balm is commonly used to relieve blisters, chapped, or cracked lips. For soft and supple hands, skin cream may be used, although it should be used in moderation. Otherwise, an oil slick may form on the instrument resulting in tongue slippage. A favorite remedy for hand chafing and chapping is a

Effect of strong foods on the kazoo.

medicated ointment originally intended for cows with chapped udders. Early on, farmers took to smearing it on themselves to alleviate their own red and raw chapped hands and faces. Kazooists use it for protection against sunburn, windburn, chafing.

Diet

Kazooists' food intake varies according to nationality, dietary customs, and personal preference. However, directly before an important performance, it is strongly recommended that abstinence from certain items be observed. Beer, chili, garlic, or other dyspeptic foods should be avoided, unless hiccoughing is a desired effect in the music.

Operating Instructions

1. Place larger end in mouth.

2. Keep fingers and thumbs out of mouth and clear of turret or other aperture areas.

3. Hum *(Don't Blow).*
   Note: If instrument fails to activate, loudly say the word *"doo"* into the larger end. Dooing into the turret may activate a particularly stubborn membrane. (If the instrument still does not respond properly, you're in trouble. You may have a broken hummer.)

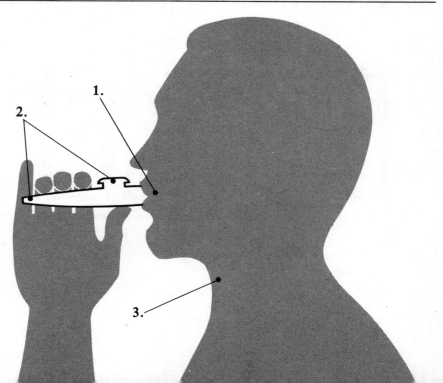

Embouchure

The embouchure, or accurate positioning of the lips, is important to correct kazooing. Assume a natural expression without smile, keeping the lips soft and flexible. Maintain that relaxed position, and open the center of the lips slightly, just enough to accommodate the kazoo.

Never exaggerate the position, as in the "Extreme Pucker" or stretch the mouth rigidly, as in the "Smile or Smirk Position."

The Smile or Smirk (incorrect)

Extreme Pucker (incorrect)

Ready Position (correct)

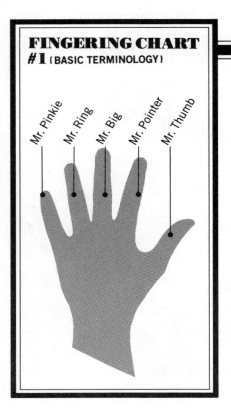

FINGERING CHART
#1 (BASIC TERMINOLOGY)

Mr. Pinkie · Mr. Ring · Mr. Big · Mr. Pointer · Mr. Thumb

Correct Hand Positions

#1—Basic

If right-handed, place the tips of the fingers of your right hand on top of the instrument, with your thumb grasping the barrel comfortably underneath. If left-handed, use the fingers of your left hand as indicated above. If ambidextrous, toss a coin.

#2—Concert Style

Place the fingers of both hands on top of the barrel, placing thumbs underneath to balance, as in Position #1.

The fingering, of course, is purely decorative, since kazoo finger holes are either nonexistent or nonfunctional.

#3—"Wah-Wah" Position

This position is often used for jazz, since it graduates the sound and varies the shading. It is more traditionally used for harmonica.

#4—"No Hands" or "Expert"

The expert kazooist may choose this position particularly during passages requiring page turning or hand choreography.

Note: Fingers are not to be placed in facial apertures adjacent to your instrument, particularly during a concert performance.

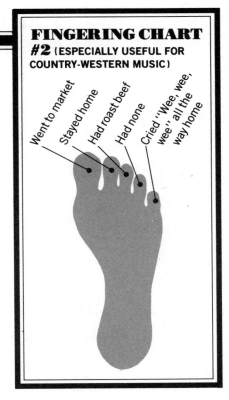

FINGERING CHART #2 (ESPECIALLY USEFUL FOR COUNTRY-WESTERN MUSIC)

Went to market
Stayed home
Had roast beef
Had none
Cried "Wee, wee, wee," all the way home

Kazooing for the Musically Marginal

To begin your mastery of kazooing, first activate your kazoo (see page 32), select a comfortable pitch, follow directions for each exercise in this section, and practice where no one else is.

The directions for refining your technique include suggested practice tunes. These songs, primarily simple tunes, are well known and part of anyone's repertoire for singing and whistling in the shower. Until you become proficient in kazoo sounds, hum the tunes into your instrument using the beginner syllables on page 39. For those who have no perceptible musical ability, take heart from the words of Ulysses S. Grant, who is reported to have said, "I only know two tunes. One of them is 'Yankee Doodle' and the other isn't." Both can be played on the kazoo.

Safety Rules for Kazooing

Place tape around the mouthpiece to prevent chipping of teeth while playing with "no-hands on."

- Do not inhale through kazoo unless passage is clear of dust, lint, or other debris.

- Never stick the kazoo up your nose. Production of the nasal tone quality is sufficient using normal methods.

- Do not walk or run while playing, unless supervised and under appropriate circumstances, such as a marching band.

- Do not persistently play the kazoo within earshot of those who are not true appreciators. It may lead to personal assault and bodily harm.

- In areas of subfreezing temperatures, use plastic model kazoos, since a metal kazoo could become permanently affixed to your lips and/or tongue.

- Avoid sticking your fingers in the

smaller end of the kazoo, unless you have very tiny fingers *or* you wish to leave the kazoo indefinitely on your tip. If stuck, you may use soap to remove the instrument, but this can cause the membrane to get soggy and also leave an unpleasant aftertaste.

- Do not use a metal kazoo outdoors during a thunderstorm or other natural phenomena accompanied by lightning.

At Home on the Kazoo Range

Speaking range bears no relationship to kazooing range. To determine your kazooing range, try singing. On the whole, most women are altos or mezzo-

sopranos and most men are baritones.

Note: For ensemble kazooing, basses are the hardest to locate. Being the most sought after tends to spoil them, making them difficult to deal with, but you'll have to put up with that if you want the full range of vocal sounds.

Pitch

The kazooist with good pitch should be forewarned that only diligent practice in listening will develop his or her ear for kazoo pitches. The expert kazooists use the "arbitrary or discretionary" pitch method. Whatever pitch you choose will result in a bombardment of sound with such complex overtones that it will be hard to tell

*Using the push-button
telephone to learn pitch can lead to
sky high phone bills*

what the original tonal center might have been. For this reason, the experienced kazooist aims for the center of the tone, makes a good approach for a lay-up, and hopes for the best on the rebound. The result is sort of a "rim shot."

The push-button telephone can be a handy practice device for beginners, since it has a limited number of pitches. Kazoo to the accompaniment of the sounds made when the buttons are pushed. If this method results in exorbitant phone bills, switch to a rotary dial and don't worry about pitch. Whenever you pull out your pocket calculator be sure to have your kazoo handy. If your calculator is the kind that has musical tones, you can practice your pitch while you do your math.

If you have no pitch whatsoever, stick with solo kazooing.

Articulation

Because of the delightfully murky quality of kazoo sonorities, articulation and clear diction are of the utmost importance to the kazooist.

Special attention and much practice should be devoted to the art of overarticulation, exaggerating the syllables to be sung, spoken, or tongued. The following is a basic vocabulary of kazoo articulation syllables for the beginner:

doo, dee, dum, da, ta, tu, tum

Once you have mastered these, you should proceed to the more advanced list of authorized kazoo sounds on page 40.

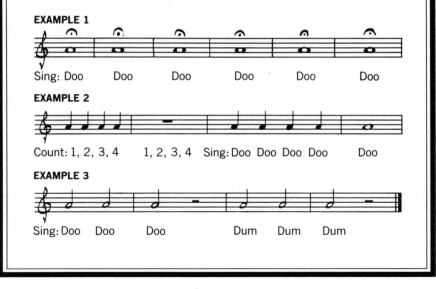

UNI-TONE PRACTICE TUNES FOR ARTICULATION

Practice examples 1 through 3. Then practice them using the sounds and articulations in the box on page 40. Any or all of the sounds may be used separately or in combination.

EXAMPLE 1

Sing: Doo   Doo   Doo   Doo   Doo   Doo

EXAMPLE 2

Count: 1, 2, 3, 4   1, 2, 3, 4   Sing: Doo Doo Doo Doo   Doo

EXAMPLE 3

Sing: Doo   Doo   Doo   Dum   Dum   Dum

AUTHORIZED LIST OF ACCEPTABLE SOUNDS AND ARTICULATIONS TO PRACTICE ON THE KAZOO

a
ach
ah
am
ap
arg
ark
arp
atch
blaft
blah
blanft
blant
blap
blat
dah
dee
doo
doom
doomp
doop
dum
ecch
echk
erg
erp
glitch
glort
glortch
glurp
ha
hee
heep
herp
hmmm-mm
hmmm-mmm
mmm
mmm
ho
hum
ich
icht
ka
karp
kritch
krrp
la
lee
li
lo
lol
lop
lul
lum
lun
lurp
mmm-mmm
moff
mom
mop
morf
morn
morp
mos
mrp
muff
mugort
mum
mump
mus
nah
nich
nit
nnn
nom
norp
nortch
num
og
oh
ooo
oop
op
org
orp
pip
pitoot
pitui
poo
poop
pop
porp
prrup
quarg
quash
que
rep
retch
rivet
romp
rop
rot
rrrp
rrrr
rrt
sam
scam
slop
slorp
slump
snag
snam
snap
snart
snat
snit
snort
sorg
sploing
sss
ssst
ta
ta-ka
tcht
ti
tra
tra-la
tretch
trrt
tst
tu-ka
tum
tum-tum
ugh
urg
utch
wa
wa wa
wirp
woo
woom
wrrp
wub
wum
wuz
ya
yoo
yub
yum
yup
zah
zeb
zedah
zen
zib
zit
zoo
zoom

Advanced Sounds:

blang
bzownt
bzznt
chank
chunka
dang
dink
dit
doik
doing
fak
fap
finitch
foidoip
foing
fong
foompt
foong
fot
furd
fwat
fween
fweep
glit
gloig
glorg
gluk
gort
gurnp
krunchle
krurkle
noit
oomph
ploin
poif
poit
pwang
shkling
skitch
skrotch
slmet
sluk
snark
snorkle
spap
splang
splork
spritz
sprong
swart
thaff
toof
turg
twing
zickik
zooka

Muting the Sound

For romantic passages in the music, or for playing in areas with noise restriction codes, it is possible to mute the sound and make the pitches *very* soft, by turning the instrument around and humming into the smaller end, using it as the mouthhole. This is not practical in fast passages where the soft pitches alternate rapidly with loud ones, since this would be too awkward. For fast passages it's best to work with a second kazooist: while you do the muted pitches into the smaller end of the kazoo, your partner plays the louder notes into the regular mouthpiece.

"Rock-a-Bye Baby" or any other lullabies make good practice tunes for muting.

Dynamics

Dynamics is the technical term for how loud or soft the sound is (musical volume). If you play the kazoo too loudly (fortissimo), the

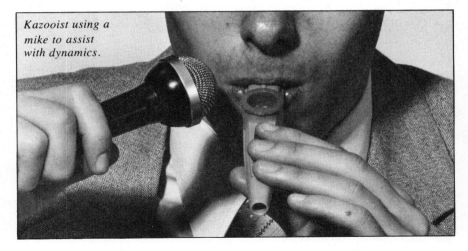

Kazooist using a mike to assist with dynamics.

membrane might break. If you play too softly (pianissimo), the membrane does not vibrate properly. So the kazooist aims for consistency in the middle dynamic range, striving always for mediocrity.

Excellent practice tunes for dynamics are "John Jacob Jingleheimer Schmidt" and "Deep in the Heart of Texas.

Vocalization

The dedicated kazooist may extend his or her range through the diligent practice of vocalization exercises. Pronounce the following syllables, first without the kazoo and then a second time pronouncing them into the instrument.

Level 1. eh ēe ah ōh ooo
Level 2. ah eh ēe ōh ooo
Level 3. ēe ī ēe ī ō

Once you have reached Level 3, you are prepared for folk and farm kazooing.

Voice Projection

Effective voice projection will enable you to reach the greatest number of listeners in the shortest period of time. When projecting their voices, opera and classical singers use head tones. Jazz and pop singers use throat and chest tones. Kazooists use anything they can.

Perform frequent repetitions of the musical scales (do, re, mi, fa, sol, la, ti, do) with the assistance of a friend or loved one. Ask your helper to keep backing away as you repeat the scales, requiring you to increase your projection so that he or she can always hear you. Helpers should not be permitted to back off into a car and drive away.

Breath Control

The basic technique for breathing is, of course, *in* and *out*. However, notes should only be produced on the *out*-take, unless you are striving for a piggy snort (page 51).

Practice exercise for breath control

1. Place a "party blowout" (the paper party favor that unrolls when you blow into it) firmly into the smaller end of the kazoo.

2. Suck in a huge breath, inhaling through the mouth (not the nose) and expanding the abdominal area. Do not raise shoulders when inhaling

3. Holding on to the party favor, blow out and sustain the breath, keeping the paper tail expanded for as long as possible.

4. If dizziness results, discontinue practice and take a vacation.

Extensive breath control practice is crucial to proper renditions of such classics as:

"I Know an Old Lady Who Swallowed a Fly"

"Green Grass Grew All Around"

"Twelve Days of Christmas"

"100 Bottles of Beer on the Wall,"

"In Poland There's an Inn"

Fry Tones

The bottom tone of the bass can be lowered (although not necessarily improved), by using a singing technique referred to as "fry tones." Pick the lowest note possible and then use the throat to pronounce the syllables, "WRahahahah," imitating the sound of a creaking door. Fry tones are useful for producing a bottom note lower than your ordinary capacity or for occasions requiring sustained growling, such as pep rallies and football games.

Vibrato

Vibrato is the wavy variation of sound within the tone that gives it texture. It adds colorful overtones by changing the sound waves and is a technique used by singers and many instrumentalists to enhance their tone quality.

Vibrato may be achieved by varying the breath using muscular control of your diaphragm (stomach) or by vibrating the lip or jaw.

An attempt should be made to keep the vibrato in even pulses, this is the most pleasant effect.

Practice exercise. The kazooist should breathe from the diaphragm, choosing a single pitch and pronouncing the syllables "ta-ah-ah" into the kazoo. This is known as the "Santa Claus laugh." It produces a wavy quality within the sound, enhancing the richness of the sonority.

Snow White's diminutive friends sing a song that the kazooist can perform to practice vibrato—"Heigh Ho, Heigh Ho, It's Off to Work We Go." "Greensleeves," Brahms's "Lullaby," and "Up on the Rooftops" may be used to practice more advanced stages.

Rhythm and Meter

Rhythm and meter are different things, but the distinction probably will not matter much to you as a solo kazooist.

For ensemble kazooing, you will need to know basic musical counting. If you do not know how long each note should last and how it fits, it can cause hostility among the members of your musical group. For example, if you hold the note too long, you will overlap onto someone else's note and end after everybody else is finished.

If you don't hold your note long enough, you will come in on the next one too soon and cause another collision situation, skipping over everybody's part to get to the end before they do.

To avoid this potential musical embarrassment, find a patient kazoo partner and practice "Row, Row, Row Your Boat" (as a round), with frequent repetitions until you have mastered musical counting. Other practice rounds include "White Coral Bells," "Make New Friends," and "Why Doesn't My Goose Sing as Well as Thy Goose." You may, instead, stick to solo kazooing where you don't have to worry about stepping on anyone else's toes, or notes.

Holding a note too long can lead to embarrassment.

Double and Triple Tonguing

Standard instrumental articulation for single tonguing (syllables you tongue into the kazoo) includes

Movement for triple tonguing.

"ta," "du," or "tu" but hardly any musician does just this for fast passages, because single tonguing cannot be reproduced quickly enough. Instead they use double or triple tonguing. Standard instrumental articulation for double tonguing is "ta-ka," "du-ka," "du-ga," or "tu-ka." Triple tonguing is just like double tonguing, only faster. Triple tonguing requires the use of an additional syllable: "ta-ka-ta," "du-ka-ta," or "du-ga-da."

This technique is crucial for the proper execution of Chopin's "Minute Waltz," which takes an expert pianist at least 98 seconds to complete. "The Fifty-Nine Second Waltz" for kazoos can be completed in as little as 55 seconds by using the double or triple tonguing technique.

Practice exercises. Choose whichever of these syllables are easiest for you to repeat, and practice the repetition, using "ta-ka," "du-ka," or "du-ga." Use any comfortable pitch.

Flutter and Slap Tonguing

Flutter tonguing is a rapid whirring of the tongue against the teeth with the sound of a rolled "thrrrrr," something like a Scotsman with his tongue stuck in a lisp. It is one of the techniques that great teachers claim either you can do or you can't, but whatever the case, it can't be taught. It doesn't seem to be related to the inherited genetic ability to curl your tongue in the center. Flutter tonguing between two pitches can create a trill-like effect. Trills are used in marching band music, specifically in standard flute and clarinet parts adapted for the kazoo. This technique is also particularly useful for bird and animal calls.

Slap tonguing is a sloppier version of flutter tonguing, which involves greatly extending your tongue while producing a much coarser sound. The "Blue Danube Waltz" is greatly enhanced by slap tonguing—dum, dee, da, da dum, THUCK-THUCK, THUCK-THUCK . . . and so forth.

Glissandos

Glissandos are transitions from one note to another through the use of a series of passing tones. The type of glissando you will use on the kazoo requires the player to gliss, smooth, or glide over all the notes between the two indicated. How you get between the two notes, whether you buzz, bend, gliss, rip, slide, or bump is of little relevance, as long as you arrive at your destination. The easiest and most successful glissando technique for the kazooist is the "smear." Simply start on the beginning note and smear up or down to the indicated target note.

Jazz and blues kazooists make regular use of the bent tone glis-

PRACTICE EXERCISES

Double Tonguing

	Ta	–	ka,	–	Ta	–	ka
or	Du	–	ga,	–	Du	–	ga
or	Du	–	ka,	–	Du	–	ka

Triple Tonguing

	Ta	–	ka	–	ta,	–	Ta	–	ka	–	ta
or	Du	–	ka	–	ta,	–	Du	–	ka	–	ta
or	Du	–	ga	–	da,	–	Du	–	ga	–	da

sando. Advanced kazooists can practice a glissando technique in Gershwin's "Rhapsody in Blue."

Balalaika Effect

The sound of the balalaika, a Russian lutelike instrument, can be simulated by tonguing on the kazoo, using either rapid repetition of the articulation "lu-lu-lu," "addle-addle-addle," or "doodle-oodle-oodle," depending on your esthetic preference.

The balalaika effect can be used as a vocal accompaniment, without kazoo, propelling the tongue outside the mouth in a rapid side-to-side rotation pronouncing the same syllables or using the pronunciation "blhlhlhlhl." Shaking the head from side to side helps keep the motion perpetual. The visual image is greatly enhanced by strumming an imaginary instrument, while producing the vocalized sounds.

"Those Were the Days" and "Song of the Volga Boatmen" are excellent practice songs for the balalaika effect.

Double Barrelled Approach (Multiple Instruments)

Because of the kazoo's size, more than one kazoo can be played at a time, provided the player's lips can wrap tightly enough around the instruments to sufficiently seal the air leakage. The use of more than one instrument looks impressive but adds little to the musicality of the moment since the single ka-

zooist can produce a maximum of one set of sounds at a time, no matter how many instruments he can accommodate in his or her mouth.

Formation of New Instruments Using

Extreme tandem kazooing.

Band Instruments and Kazoos

The kazoo can effectively be used as a mouthpiece on any standard brass instrument. The tuba with kazoo mouthpiece becomes a kazooba, the baritone horn becomes a zaritone, the bugle becomes a bazoogle, the trumpet becomes a trumpoo, the French horn becomes a French hornazoo, and so on. The kazoo can also be used as a mouthpiece for certain woodwind instruments, such as clarinet (clarizoo) or saxophone (saxophoo).

Tandem Kazooing

For additional amplification, two or three kazoos may be taped together, end on end, to form one long tube with multiple turrets. The addition of a funnel at the end of the tube will further enhance the sound projection, acting acoustically as the bell of a brass or wind instrument does to disseminate sound emitting from the end of the tube.

Utilitarian Kazoo Effects

(From the Birds to the Bees)

There are several kazoo sounds that serve to delight the kazooist, while at the same time accomplishing a useful function by calling birds or animals. In the mouth of an accomplished kazooist, this can be achieved with astonishing success.

If you are extremely expert at imitation, you should be aware that you may attract not only the intended target, but also end up luring in a number of befuddled hunters, who have mistaken your call for the real thing. For this reason, in calling any sort of game birds or hunting prey, it is important to exercise great caution to avoid being shot or bagged yourself.

Bird Calls

- Chicken sounds can be made using the syllables "errach, bawlk, bawlk." It's best to perform the bawlk beginning on a low pitch with the "b" and raising to a higher pitch for the throat-catching "awlk."

- An "rrrr-rr-rr-rr-errr" repetition will give you the barnyard wake-up call, a rooster's cry.

- The sea gull can easily be imitated by the kazooist performing a screaming "$\overline{\text{eee}}$" starting on the high pitch and trailing off in a downward bent pitch.

Turkey Calling

Here's a handy seasonal call, popular every Thanksgiving. A double or single reed (free mirliton) turkey caller is commercially available, but a skilled kazooist can achieve a perfectly satisfactory call.

The turkey aficionado is able to produce the entire turkey repertoire on kazoo, including huffing, yelps, putts, purrs, clucks, whistles, kee-kee run, cackle, and the ever popular gobble.

The easiest call to master is the basic "bllullulp," pronouncing the sound rapidly on a high pitch. This call in itself is sufficient to call any domestic and most wild turkeys.

It is important to note that turkey calling should not be attempted in the rain. Turkeys are so stupid that when they look up to find the caller, they do so with open mouths and can drown as a result. Rain also results in soggy vibrators for the kazooist, or even rust, so on the whole, it is best to wait for more favorable weather conditions.

Piggy Snort

This sound should be practiced for extended periods of time as penance for overindulging at the dinner table. The piggy snort is achieved by inhaling sharply through the nose to produce a nasal snort in imitation of the pig sound.

It is most useful for imitation of the drum, to produce roll-offs at the beginning of marches or other drum/percussive effects within the music. Those who are musically tutored in percussion can effec-

tively imitate paradiddles, single or double strokes, and 5, 7, 9, or even 11 stick rolls.

Frog Noises

You don't need to have green flippers to sound as if you've been

around a swamp. To achieve a truly fine tree frog sound requires a soprano kazooist, although lower voices can approximate the effect in falsetto. The sound is made by the articulation "brrreep," rolled on a flutter tongue from a lower pitch up to top pitch and repeated two or three times. Other frog sounds like "brrap," "rrrack," and "churrgarrroom" are better suited to the bass kazooist.

One note of caution: overdoing these sounds should be avoided since it may cause warts on the vocal cords.

Donkey Call

You will probably never have use for a donkey call—that is, unless you go prospecting for gold. Inhale on the syllable "hee," exhale on "haw" for an effective donkey call. The "Grand Canyon Suite" by Grofé uses this effect nicely, as do several folk songs, of which "Old MacDonald Had a Farm" is the best known. Use the inhale/exhale technique for the "hee-haw" syllables. Once you remember, "Here a hee" (inhale on hee), "Here a haw" (exhale on haw), the rest is easy.

Moose Call

If you should ever be in the situation of needing to find a mate for a lovelorn moose, your kazoo can come in handy. Commercially made moose callers may be purchased, but a perfectly acceptable sound can be achieved with a kazoo.

Before commencing, it is important to check your immediate area of the woods for moose in close proximity, and take care not to stand in the center of a path when calling.

The call itself is an extended "Ououhooohh." The initial bellow begins on a low pitch, rising slightly and then dropping in descending scale on the final "ooohh." The ending sometimes

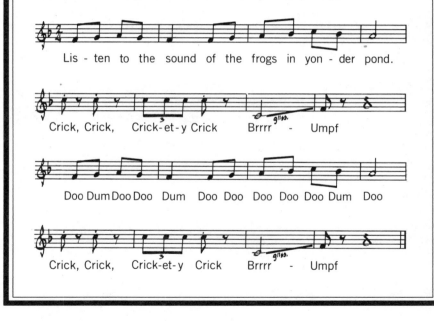

FROGGY PRACTICE TUNE

Sing the lyrics the first time through. Kazoo the second time. This may be used as a solo or a three-part round.

Lis - ten to the sound of the frogs in yon - der pond.

Crick, Crick, Crick-et-y Crick Brrrr - Umpf

Doo Dum Doo Doo Dum Doo Doo Doo Doo Doo Dum Doo

Crick, Crick, Crick-et-y Crick Brrrr - Umpf

drops slowly, sometimes more sharply, and closely resembles the cry of a large wolf with a bass voice and severe intestinal difficulty.

The Bzst and the Zzt

Some experts claim that bees and kazooists both hum because they don't know the words. Whatever the reason, bee sounds are a natural on the kazoo. The "bzst" sound is begun with the "b," quickly moving on to the "zst" syllable while the tongue vibrates in the central mouth cavity behind closed teeth. You must be careful not to cut off the air stream with the vibrating tongue.

For the "zzt" the experienced buzzer can begin a "zz" on a se-

lected pitch and sharply accent the rise of the "t" part of the sound on a pitch a half step higher. The most eloquent use of this technique is in "Flight of the Bumblebee," which has a stunning arrangement by Kazoophony (see page 86), "Plight of the Kazoomble Bee," scored for solo

kazooist, soprano kazoomble bee, and repercussionist. *Note:* It is important for the amateur not to practice too close to outdoor hive areas, since human understanding of bee language is still in its infancy and one can't tell how the bees might construe what is communicated.

Novelty Kazooing

This category is largely experimental in nature and is useful mostly for free form party kazooing or novelty effects. Some may be added into musical compositions for emphasis, but generally these noises are used as sound effects rather than melodically employed.

The Doppler Effect

The Doppler effect is an apparent change in the frequency of the sound waves, which occurs when the source of the sound and the receiver of the sound are in motion relative to one another.

The kazooist can achieve this effect in one of two ways:

1. The kazooist remains stationary

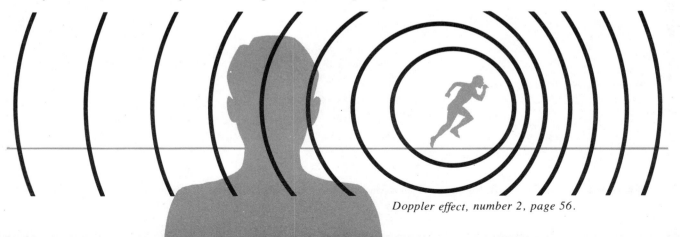

Doppler effect, number 2, page 56.

SECONDARY USES FOR THE KAZOO

1. To snuff out candles.
2. To replace stolen hood ornaments on Rolls-Royces.
3. As a pestle (or is it mortar?) for grinding corn.
4. For starting fires (use two wooden kazoos, a magnifying glass, and a boy scout).
5. As splints for small animals with injured legs.
6. As alarms for inexpensive smoke detectors.
7. As xylophones (made by lashing kazoos together and hitting them with Tootsie Pops).
8. As miniature napkin rings.
9. As a lightning rod, when placed (without kazooist) on top of a tree or barn.
10. To lead cavalry charges in military units without buglers.
11. As taxi horns in underdeveloped countries.
12. As a helmet adornment for very tiny Vikings (two kazoos required).
13. As peanut butter or other sandwich spreaders.
14. As fly swatters for people with excellent eye-hand coordination.

and recreates the illusion of approaching then receding sound by starting off softly; raising the pitch and intensity; finally fading off as if into the distance.

2. The listener remains stationary. The kazooist starts off a distance away and runs past the listener, keeping the sound at the same level throughout.

Note: The second approach is not recommended for kazooists since it requires more physical conditioning than the first and involves some risk to the kazooist's well-being if he or she should stumble.

Sirens

American siren noises require a

low pitched whine ("rrrr") for the beginning, scooping up to a higher pitch and dropping back to fade out.

The European siren is a different sound entirely, encompassing two pitches rotated back and forth. Using the basic articulation "$\overline{ee}$-ah, $\overline{ee}$-ah," the European version begins on a middle pitch with the "$\overline{ee}$" sound, then drops down in pitch on the syllable "ah" and continue rotating monotonously between the two pitches "$\overline{ee}$-ah, $\overline{ee}$-ah," and so on.

To accompany the siren with the Doppler effect, begin either siren series softly (pianissimo), gradually increasing the volume until you fade off into the distance. This is a lot of fun at parties, but should

Secondary Uses, continued

15. As air pipes for people 5 feet 8 inches to use when walking in 5 feet 10 inches of water.

16. As replacement fasteners for elongated keg-type buttons on duffel coats.

17. As nose makeup for Cyrano de Bergerac role.

18. As roach motels.

19. As a conversation piece at cocktail parties, taking into consideration the possibility of ending further conversation.

20. As warning buzzers for basketball games at schools where budgets do not permit electronic scoreboards.

21. As a sanitary mouthpiece to syphon gas during an energy crisis.

22. As amplifiers for hearing through walls, when no glass or stethoscope is available.

23. As a pasta shaper.

KAZOO SERVICE AND REPAIR CHART

CONDITION: KAZOO FAILS TO OPERATE.

POSSIBLE CAUSE	CORRECTION
1. **Incorrect starting technique by operator.**	1. **HUM . . . DO NOT BLOW! Repeat the word "Doo" again and again into the larger end of the instrument to elicit response.**
2. **Defective vibrator.**	2. **For metal kazoos: Unscrew turret, remove old vibrator. Replace with new unit. For plastic kazoos: Toss instrument and replace with one that works.**
3. **Diaphragm in upside down (metal only).**	3. **Remove turret, check diaphragm making sure *smooth* side is *down* in the annulus. Side with raised cardboard edge must face *up* toward the turret.**

not be used outdoors where it could cause a traffic hazard.

The new electronic sirens pose a challenge to all but the most expert kazooists.

Fog Horn Sound

The fog horn is most effective for the bass kazooist. The "bah-ahh-ahh" articulation begins on a low pitch with the "bah," extending above to "ahh" and returning to the tonic (the same note you started on) with the second "ahh." This is repeated over and over and again at five second intervals.

Kazooists in coastal areas may want to check with local authorities to be sure that simulating fog horns will not be confusing to ships or violate any maritime ordinances.

Water Noises

By placing the smaller end of the kazoo barrel into water and playing into the wide end a pleasing array of unusual effects can be achieved. Burbling, bubbling and excellent "grracks," "bllups" (with rolled l's) in addition to throat-produced gargling noises, such as "guh," "gah," and vibrated g's are some useful water noises.

Do not inhale when your kazoo is submerged since it ruins the membrane. The soggy vibrator will preclude any repetition of effective kazoo sounds after the intake.

The Bronx Cheer

The Bronx cheer is a sound usually used in crowds to indicate disapproval (it is also known as the rasp-

Kazoo Service Chart, continued

4. Operator has thumb or fingers over end hole.	4. Uncover the end. Try playing with no hands.
5. Operator has thumb on vibrator.	5. Remove thumb from turret.
6. Dented body.	6. Check for dents on body and turret. Call your insurance adjuster. Take to body shop for estimate before ordering repairs.
7. Broken hummer.	7. Replace kazooist.

CONDITION: ERRATIC IDLE (MISFIRE).

POSSIBLE CAUSE	CORRECTION
1. Gas (belching).	1. Try an antacid.
2. Hiccoughs.	2. Place paper grocery bag on head. Breathe in and out
3. Wrong place in music (for group kazooists).	3. Sit out until the next piece.

berry). It is particularly useful in the stands at baseball or football games. On kazoo, the technique requires an overbite in the kazoo embouchure, with the upper lip on top of the uptilted kazoo, the lower lip tucked under, and the tongue in the barrel of the kazoo. The kazooist buzzes the lips and tongue, pronouncing a motorized "th" sound, propelled forward by the vibrating lips and tongue.

Hand choreography for the Bronx cheer is simple. Place your thumbs at the sides of your head and wiggle your fingers. An alternate

thumb position is careful placement of the right or left thumb on the top of your nose and vigorously waving the fingers of that hand in a rippling effect to accompany the raspberry.

Motor Noises

"Brroom," "brrum" and so on, with rolled articulation can be used in endlessly varied motor imitations. Also useful is the throat squeal, the unrolled "rrrrr" sound familiar to any motorist who has ever slammed on the brakes for an abrupt stop in traffic. Explosion or smashing notes may also be added to this sequence of special effects.

All of these are aided by the artful use of the microphone, especially the explosion sound, usually produced by the rolling and blowing out of the syllable, "prrwh," exploding the "prrr" and continuing to taper off with the softer "whwhwh" blowing sound.

The double-handed Bronx cheer.

SPECIAL INTEREST KAZOOING

Choosing a Direction

The final step for kazooists is deciding in what direction to kazoo.

Kazooing cuts across all cultural, political, and economic barriers, and is appropriate to all ages. The range and possibility for kazoo groups is virtually limitless. It seems to vary only according to the imagination and inclination of the kazooists.

Although kazooists may choose to join a group to form a more perfect union, freedom of choice in kazooing is held to be self-evident. The rights of the individual kazooist, including the rights to free speech, to following Kazoodaism as a way of life, the right to assemble, and the assurance of a speedy and fair trial for any violation of local ordinances are guaranteed by law, at least for American kazooists. The independent kazooist who chooses individual expression rather than kazooing in a group is to be taken just as seriously as the group kazooist. The domestic kazooist who chooses to remain at home, in the kitchen, or with the children, is to be no less respected than the ensemble or professional (working) kazooist. Freedom of kazooing is the rule, rather than the exception.

Impromptu Kazoo Groups

Impromptu kazoo groups are springing up everywhere, at parties, rallies, and conventions, and wherever people gather for fun. Longevity of the group is generally dependent on the length of the event or the arrival of law enforcement officials to require compliance with local noise ordinances.

The following two songs and one cheer are the basics to know for impromptu kazooing occasions.

Birthday Party Serenade. Place a paper "blow-out" in the smaller end of a kazoo and tape it to hold it in place. Kazoo the first verse to "Happy Birthday to You," using articulation as follows:

Verse #1
(kazooed)

Doo Dee Doo Doo Doo Doo
Doo Dee Doo Doo Doo Doo
Doo Dee Doo Doo Doo Dee Doo
Doo Dee Doo Doo Doo Doo.

Verse #2
(sung; adapt tune slightly to accommodate lyrics)

Happy birthday to you
I'm kazooing to you
I wish you a happy birthday
What more can I say?

Impromptu kazooing often helps to get partygoers into the correct mood.

New Year's Eve Traditional. Place paper "blow-out" mechanism in the smaller end of a kazoo and tape it securely in place. Sing the first verse to the tune of "Auld Lang Syne." Kazoo the chrorus. When finished kazooing for the evening, carefully remove paper "blow-out" and put away in storage for use at birthday occasions or for next New Year's.

Verse:

Should auld acquaintance
   be forgot
And never brought to
   mind?
I've lost him (her) once
   again, I fear
Maybe I'll find him (her)
   here next year.

*Chorus:**

Dah Dah Dah Dah Dah Dah Bah Dah
Dah Dah Dah Dah Bah Dah
Bah Dah Bah Dah Bah Dah Bah Dah
Dah Dah Dah Bah Dah Dah Dah

---

*"For Auld Lange Syne, my dear," etc. are the normal lyrics here.

Kazoo Bands

Kazoo bands are probably the most popular form of group kazooing. They appear in great variety, from preschool, elementary school and recreation department bands (where the level of skill is questionable, but the style exuberant), on through the high school level and college (where the skills are no better, but the participants are older).

Band uniforms vary as widely as the bands. Regulation band uniforms are sometimes used, but more often T-shirts are emblazoned with appropriate slogans.

Even more important than the membership or the musical skill of individual marchers is the acquisition of a distinctive band name.

The 39th Street Kazoo Marching Band and Sis Boom Bah Chorus

The "Red, White, and Kazoo Band,"® and the "Kazoovatory Drum and Bagel Corps" are two possibilities. One of the more interesting groups, "The 19th Ward Community Association Fully Integrated Affirmative Action Kazoo Marching Band" began in Rochester, New York, in 1974, led by kazoo guru, Bob Larter. As they progressed in experience (although not in skill), they added the "Electric Drill Team and Auxiliary." With an intensive five minute practice session, they marched without personal injury, playing kazoos and carrying cordless electric drills. No recognizable patterns, formations, or even traditions seem to have resulted.

Practice exercise for a kazoo band (marching or otherwise). Sing the verse to the tune of "Waltzing Matilda." Kazoo on the refrain, to the same tune, using the syllables "doo" and "dee" as indicated.

Verse 1.

As I was a-walkin
A-walking down that
  country road
I heard the sound
  of a lonely kazoo
So I picked up my
  feet
And I started marchin'
  to the beat
Then I just joined in
  that doo doo dee doo

Refrain (kazoo):

Doo Doo Dee Doo Doo
Doo Doo Dee Doo Doo
Doo Doo Dee Doo Doo Dee Doo
  Doo Dee Doo
Doo Doo Doo Doo Doo Doo Doo
  Dee Doo Dee Doo Doo Dee
  Doo
Doo Doo Dee Doo Doo Dee Doo
  Doo Dee Doo

Verse 2.

So the two of us was
  marchin'
A-marchin' down that country
  road
Up comes another man
A-playing kazoo
So he picked up his feet
And he started marchin'

to that beat
Then he just joined
   in the doo doo dee doo

(Refrain)

Verse 3.

So we kept on a-marchin'
A-marchin' down
   that country road
Soon we had joined
   up a whole bloomin'
   band (Ain't it grand)
So we picked up our feet
And we kept on marchin'
   to that beat

Please wontcha join us
   in doo doo dee doo

(Refrain)

(At end, fade out on last line
   of "dee" and "doos")

A first kazoo encounter.

Children's Groups

It is believed by some that we are all born with the innate ability to kazoo. If left uncultivated, we lose the ability sometime around puberty. Therefore, children are naturals, but for safety reasons, children under the age of three should not be allowed to kazoo unless carefully supervised.*

*Common sense tells any responsible adult that children under the age of three shouldn't do much of anything that's unsupervised, so this should not create any particular hardship.

Arranging Music for Kazoo

If the music has no spaces (rests) between the notes, this leaves no place to breathe. If the notes extend too high or too low for your singing range, then you are also in trouble. Certain adjustments must be made to accommodate these problems, such as adding rests, bending the rhythm, or juxtaposing notes into more convenient octaves. Kazooists call this arranging. Musical purists call this atrocious.

Melody and Harmony

In the study of music, great amounts of space are allotted to dissertation on musical form. For the purpose of kazooing, it would probably suffice to describe melody as notes in a horizontal line. When they are piled up vertically, they make a chord. In kazoo music, a chord presumes there is more than one kazooist. Otherwise, it is not a possibility. If the chord is pleasing, it is harmony; if it is not pleasing, it is dischord. Anyone wishing to dispute the technical accuracy of this should feel free to do so, keeping in mind, however, that there is only so much technical jargon the ordinary kazooist can tolerate and still be able to function. Oversimplification is always dangerous, but in this case, absolutely essential.

Written Kazoo Music

If you can't read regular music, you can't read kazoo music either. The classic diatonic scale is based on the "do-re-me-fa-sol-la-ti-do" tones, as most folks learned from "The Sound of Music." If there is more than one kazooist, some semblance of this tonal system will be required. For this reason, you will either need to hum by yourself or else learn to follow conventional organized musical patterns. If you are musically untutored, you will have to improvise or do the best you can with uni-tone kazooing.

ESSENTIAL MUSIC NOTATION

Space does not allow for an entire course in music theory,
but there are a few basics that kazooists should know:

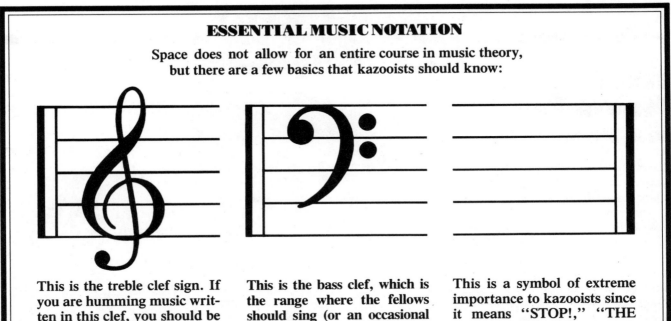

This is the treble clef sign. If you are humming music written in this clef, you should be female, a male doing falsetto, or a 17th-century castrato.

This is the bass clef, which is the range where the fellows should sing (or an occasional female, such as Carol Channing or the like).

This is a symbol of extreme importance to kazooists since it means "STOP!," "THE END," "IT'S OVER!"

Rock Kazooing

The kazooist who is into '50s-style rock 'n' roll, folk-rock, hard rock, disco, punk, or new wave will be pleased to note that the kazoo adapts easily to any of these styles.

The most famous rock kazooist was Richard Starkey, although he did not kazoo much until after he changed his name to Ringo Starr. "You're Sixteen" was a number-one hit in January, 1974, with Ringo as featured kazooist. Rock groups such as "The Lovin' Spoonful" and "Brooklyn Bridge" also used kazoos. Although none of these groups are still in existence, the kazoo was probably not

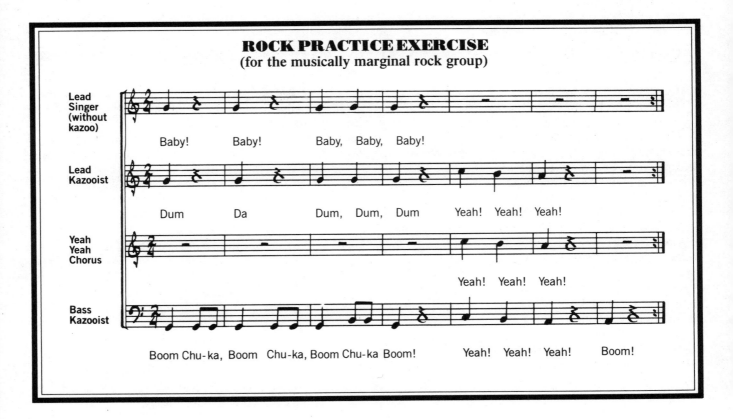

instrumental in their breakup.

The basic problem for rock kazooists is acquiring an excellent rhythmic accompaniment. For the beginner, or a group that can't afford an expert drummer it is best to kazoo along with rock tapes or records, doubling the melody or rhythmic parts that strike your fancy. For disco a percussive effect can be made by the kazooist, using the syllable "ch" or "tch," to emphasize the disco beat.

Note: When using electronic devices to amplify rock kazoo music, kazooists should take steps to preserve their hearing. The timbre of the kazoo vibrations (along with those of associated accompanying instruments), can cause severe damage to the ear, resulting in the loss of the thousands of tiny internal hairs that aid hearing. Therefore, to prevent bald ears, the kazooist is encouraged to wear prophylactic earplugs.

It is probably also judicious for the electrified kazooist to have dry lips and wear rubber soled shoes. Further, *never* play outside during inclement weather (heavy dew or rain).

Fabulous fifties rock practice exercise scored for the musically marginal rock group. Your group should consist of a:

Lead singer (no kazoo)
Lead kazooist
Yeah-Yeah chorus (2 or more kazooists)
Bass kazooist

Perform all together as an ensemble. Repeat the following as often as can be tolerated.

Top line: Lead singer does lyrics, with expression, but without kazoo.

Second line: Lead kazooist articulates on the syllables "dum dah."

Third line: Yeah-Yeah chorus (with kazoos) rests until they come in at fifth bar. The "yeah-yeah" is articulated through the kazoos and should be as nasal as possible, pronounced way up in the nose.

Bottom line: Bass kazooist may play up an octave or two, depending on how low a range he or she has. Articulate on syllables "boom-chuk-ka." Join the Yeah-Yeah chorus at bar five and end with "boom."

Jazz Techniques

Jazz requires improvising around a melody, leading some critics to refer to jazz as "musical doodling." If you are musical, probably the best approach to jazz is to listen carefully to good performers and imitate their styles. Learning scat singing is an excellent approach to acquiring good jazz kazoo technique.

If you are not musical, play with loud backup recordings. Softly play along as background music with the tape or record playing, making an attempt to blend in in the least offensive manner.

Written music for jazz looks like other music, except you refer to it as "charts," not scores. If you can't read music, try wearing sunglasses (shades) during a performance. You will not be able to see well, but at least you will look right for the part.

Art Grider, Memphis State University Photo Services

One simple blues technique which the amateur can practice is bending notes. Basically, you go for the note, miss it by hitting underneath it and then slide back to get it. This creates a sort of swooping effect that is readily recognizable in jazz circles. Simple tunes, such as "I've Been Working on the Railroad" can be made to sound much more interesting, when using this technique. The expert may wish to go on to adapt Gershwin into "Rhapsody in Kazoo," using note-bending with spectacular effect in the opening clarinet solo. "When the Saints Go Marching In" and "In the Mood" are two good jazz practice tunes.

Dixieland is also highly adaptable, especially if you combine the kazoo with a banjo and a tuba, or tuba with kazoo mouthpiece (kazooba), trombone and piano. This type of jazz requires some creative improvisation from the proficient player. It may also be kazooed at its more basic level, by simply humming the melody line of such classics as "Has Anybody Seen My Gal?" which offers innumerable opportunities to rhyme lines with kazoo (blue, two, and so on).

Jazz practice exercise scored for the barely adequate jazz quartet.
Your group should consist of a:
  Lead kazooist
  Wah-Wah chorus (2 or more kazooists)
  Bass kazooist

Play together in ensemble, repeating as you feel like it.

Top line: Lead kazooist does glissando, starting on bottom note (G) and smearing all the notes together to slide up under to the top note (C). The articulation used for the glissando is "Oh, yeah." After the "du-wah" is a spoken "yeah!" (without kazoo).

Middle line: Wah-Wah chorus uses hands in shading position (see page 35) to cover and uncover the kazoo on each "wah" to create a jazz effect on the "wah-wahs."

Bass line: Play in the lowest octave comfortable for you. Your "doo da wop wops" are in syncopated rhythm, so make the first "wop" longer than the second to create the proper rhythmic figure.

Country Kazooing

The sound and lyrics for country and western music are generated well up into the nose. Famous country kazooists include Jimmie Rodgers, Gene Autry, and numerous jug and washboard band people who recorded in the 1920s and '30s. Also not to be forgotten are Belly Joe and Jelly Dough Kaminsky of Kazoophony's* Kaminsky Country Singers.

In addition to bands composed entirely of kazoos, there are many musical ensembles that use the kazoo with other instrumentation. Possible groups include jug and kitchen bands; hokum, skiffle, and shuffle bands; and country string bands.

The instrumentation in each of these groups varies according to the group needs. Some commonly used instruments appropriate to use in combination with kazoos for these ensembles are the washtub bass, comb-and-tissue-paper, finger cymbals, spoons, folk harp, banjo, and guitar.

Do-it-yourself country kazoo practice tune. To make your own country song, use the lyrics included here, and combine them in any order you choose. Use a tune of your choice.

---

*For more on Kazoophony, see page 86.

Sample lyrics:

"Ah love _____"
(choose one):
you
ma dawg
beer

"Ah've lost _____"
(choose one):
ma love
ma dawg
ma mind

"Ah've found _____"
(any of the above):

"You've broke _____"
(choose one):
ma heart
ma truck
ma arm

Country and western tune for the moderately excellent kazooist. Kazooists follow the music, as written. Lead singer (without kazoo) uses country twang and sticks the words and pitch up his or her nose. Guitar accompaniment helps add ''atmosphere'' and makes it sound a lot better.

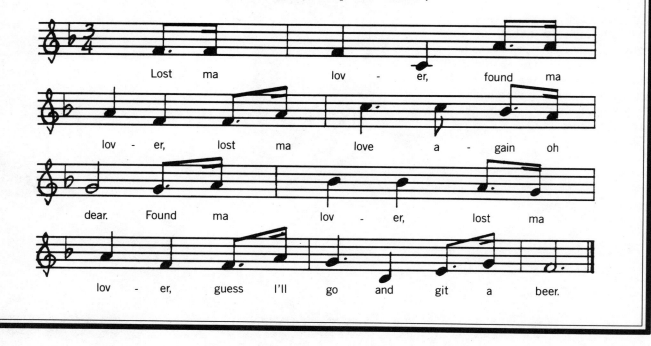

COUNTRY PRACTICE EXERCISE
(for the modestly adequate kazooist)

Lost ma lov - er, found ma

lov - er, lost ma love a - gain oh

dear. Found ma lov - er, lost ma

lov - er, guess I'll go and git a beer.

Classical Kazooing

Within his or her own abilities, the expert musician may adapt any of the classics. The rich contrapuntal texture of John Philip Sousa marches converts easily to ensemble kazooing, as evidenced by the many "John Philip Kazooza" adaptations done by the world's premier kazoo ensemble, Kazoophony.* Their favorite is "The Stars and Stripes Forever and Ever . . . and Ever," which uses coloratura soprano as the piccolo solo and liberally applies flutter tonguing (see page 46) to the trills.

*For more on Kazoophony, see page 86.

*For more on Kazoophony, see page 86.

SYMPHONIC KAZOOING

Leonard Bernstein, a man of rare insight and vision, has brought symphonic kazooing to audiences on more than one occasion, but the kazoo has only begun to make inroads in the symphonic world.

The most successful symphonic kazooing has been accomplished by Kazoophony, in its program "Music vs. Noise." Performances with the Syracuse Symphony, Tulsa Philharmonic, Erie Youth Orchestra, and the San Antonio Symphony have all been more successful than would seem possible.

"Eine Kleine Nachtmusik" by Mozart also transfers easily to kazoo in the Kazoophony arrangement entitled "I'm Inclined to Kazoomusik" by Wolfgang Amadeus Mozartsky. It uses the string quartet arrangement for four-part kazoo harmony, with a percussion part added to enhance the beat. For kazooists, the second or slow movement is generally omitted since kazoo resonance does not lend itself well to extended lyrical passages. It tends to change the timbre to irritating tone color long before the notes end.

Classical Kazooing Practice Exercises

The following is a practice exercise for classical kazooing.

For this exercise, unless you have perfect pitch (or you don't care what key you are in), you will need a pitch pipe or piano to give the starting pitch for each part.

Classical practice exercise for the uni-tone kazooist. This exercise, based on the Beermeister-Singer's Song from "Tannheuser Busch," can be mastered by kazooists of limited range and experience (one-note agility). Count the rests carefully, beating with your foot, if necessary.

If you should happen upon an 80-piece orchestra and an operatic cast with the rest of the musical score, this composition could be performed in its entirety. (Due to cultural arts budget restrictions, we were not able to publish all of the orchestra parts here. This is the kazoo transcription of the fifth-horn part only.)

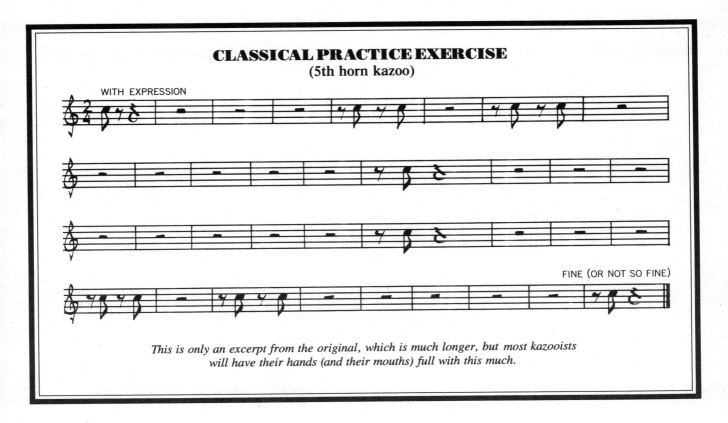

CLASSICAL PRACTICE EXERCISE
(5th horn kazoo)

*This is only an excerpt from the original, which is much longer, but most kazooists
will have their hands (and their mouths) full with this much.*

One Final Note (♪)

You have now been thoroughly immersed in the history and background of your instrument and are versed in its technique. You are ready to kazoo with pride.

However, before you go, a word of caution: Although kazoo playing is not fattening, nor is it injurious to your health, it is only fair to warn you that it may be habit-forming . . . ''

Kazoos and Their Cousin

ARTISAN'S KAZOO
This has a hand-hewn, wooden superstructure. The kazoo swings open laterally to allow replacement of the resonator, which is centrally located in the instrument's interior. (Harmony-In-Wood, Rochester, N.Y.)

WALT DISNEY MICKEY MOUSE KAZOO®
Amusing miniature Mickey Mouse figure with megaphone. All plastic construction, with wide circular mouthpiece is especially well suited to the facial structure of the preschooler. (Quaker Oats Company)

HI-FI OR AMPLIFIER KAZOO
This was also known in the 1940s as a "Kazoophone." An enlarged horn-shaped bell attached to the turret markedly amplifies the volume and channels the sound. (Kazoo Company, Inc.)

HUM-A-ZOO®
The Hum-a-Zoo® is a close relative, but not identical to the standard kazoo. It was first patented in 1923 and is still manufactured by Trophy Music, Inc. of Cleveland, Ohio.

GOLD PLATED KAZOO
Known as the "Humdinger," it is made of metal plated with 24K gold. Plating does not perceptibly alter the tone quality, but it does raise the status and the retail price. (S. J. Miller, Boulder, Colo.)

SILVER KAZOO
A three-inch sterling silver kazoo, with replaceable wax paper resonator. A top-of-the-line kazoo, it is acoustically excellent for the soprano voice. (Distributor, Lenor Doskow, silversmith, Montrose, N.Y.)

CLARINET KAZOO
A 10½-inch metal instrument, with gold finish and red plastic safety mouthpiece. Perforated finger holes serve only as decoration. (Kazoo Company, Inc.)

BUGLE KAZOO
A foot-long, heavyweight metal bugle. It has a gold finish, with red plastic safety mouthpiece and red decorative tassle. A bugle-shaped resonating chamber produces sound suitable for wake-up duty or military alert. (Kazoo Company, Inc.)

SLIDE TROMBONE KAZOO
A metal kazoo, with gold lacquer finish and red plastic safety mouthpiece. It has a movable slide which extends size from 11 to 13½ inches, but does not musically affect the instrument.

CORNET KAZOO
A metal kazoo with red plastic keys that press down and spring back. It has a gold finish, with red plastic safety mouthpiece. (Kazoo Company, Inc.)

Kazoophony, the World's Largest Quartet

Described by *The Wall Street Journal* as "America's Premier Kazoo Group," Kazoophony brings professional kazooing to its very zenith.* Spawned in the shadow of the Eastman School of Music in Rochester, N.Y., the group was founded in 1973 to encourage the art of kazoo playing, and to promote musical enrichment throughout the world.

The remarkable and widely ignored Kazoophony is a unique musical group which spoofs the formality and ritual surrounding music, while taking its kazooing seriously. It presents a hilarious theatrical evening (with choreography), combining kazoo with traditional instruments (such as trombone, piano, and percussion), and less traditional ones (such as kazooba, face and teeth playing, and operatic coloratura yodeling). Kazoophony enthusiastically assaults all forms of music.

Kazoophony has appeared extensively on television ("Tonight Show," "Mike Douglas") and on radio, at Lincoln Center and Town Hall in New York, as guest artists with symphony orchestras, at innumerable colleges and festivals . . . and at the opening of the new Yellow Trucking Company at the site of the Emerson Street Dump in Rochester, N.Y.

They have also been banned twice in Great Britain without having done anything rude that they knew about.

Kazoophony originally performed as the 80-piece Ludakravian Philharmonic . . . until budget cuts, when they were reduced to a six-person kazoo quartet. (The usual number for a kazoo quartet is seven people, so they are still missing one person.) Casting is by audition only. Artists must have conservatory training, preferably with symphonic background. All kazooists must double in characterizations and instruments.

---

*Glowing descriptions of Kazoophony are barely influenced at all by the author's 11-year involvement as leader and kazoo-keeper for the group.

Kazoophony

John Stanton

David Perlman

Kazooperman

Kazoodaphiles

For those who wish to admire as well as play the kazoo, there are opportunities for fans and groupies. Leader of the Kazoophony Fan Club is Kazooperman, a dedicated kazoo aficionado who lives in San Francisco. Fans who wish to join the Kazoophony Fan Club may write to the Kazoophony Fan Club, c/o Workman Publishing, 1 West 39 Street, New York, N.Y. 10018.

Modern Political History: Kazoo As U.S. National Instrument

America already has a national bird, a national song . . . and a national debt. It may not need those either, but why not make the kazoo the national instrument? "Tippie-canoe and play your kazoo." "Two kazoos in every garage" . . .

The kazoo is a natural choice for an American national instrument, since it is one of a very small number of instruments native to America. An exhaustive search reveals that in addition to the kazoo, the other authentic American instruments are the Sousaphone (named after John Philip Sousa),

the glass harmonica (invented by Benjamin Franklin), and the Iroquois water drum (invented by the Iroquois). The kazoo clearly should be the front-runner in this group.

For some time, an attempt has been made to make the kazoo the American national instrument. In 1976, a resolution was proposed by Midge Costanza (former aide to Jimmy Carter) and unanimously passed by the city council in Rochester, N.Y. In 1977, the vice-mayor of New York City issued a proclamation in favor of the nationalization of the kazoo. It has received much bipartisan support and the cause of the kazoo was taken by actor Paul Newman. In 1976, he signed an endorsement to make the kazoo the national instrument to "keep America humming." He was quick to say that the reason he would not be attending kazoo concerts was not because he was unappreciative of culture, but because they conflicted with his regular bowling night.

The campaign on behalf of the kazoo continues, and is now at a stage described by onlookers as "dormant." This is undoubtedly due to the economy and to the politically amorphous attitudes of dedicated kazooists who wander off and practice, rather than campaign.

Discography

Included here is a partial listing of recordings for the dedicated kazoo fan.

Classical Kazoo Recordings

Kazoophony, 1975. A live performance of a Kazoophony Concert at Cornell University, recorded while the group was being attacked by a pack of campus dogs. A collector's item,* never released for general distribution.

Kazoophony, 1978 (Aquitaine Records, Toronto). Another collector's item* distributed by CBS of Canada and for reasons clear only to those versed in international kazoo bureaucracy . . . never released in the United States.

John Menihan

Other Kazoo Recordings**

American Skiffle Bands (recorded in Alabama, Texas, and Tennessee). Folkways Records, Album No. FA2610, copyright 1957.

It's a Good Place To Go, Bottle Up and Go, Hamminie Nixon. High Water Recording Company #416.

The Great Jug Bands, Origin Jazz Library OJL-4. 12″ LP, reissues.

Memphis Jug Band, recorded in Memphis, 1928, Ben Ramey, kazoo.

Harmonicas, Washboards, Fiddles and Jugs, Roots RL-311. 12″ LP, reissues.

---

*The collector's item designation indicates an outstanding recording, which is unavailable to anyone who might want it, including those in the group that made it.

**Listen to kazoo appearances on recordings of Spike Jones, Gene Autry, the Hoosier Hot Shots, Jimmy Rodgers, P.D.Q. Bach, and Ringo Starr.

"Banjo Joe" (Gus Cannon) on kazoo, recorded in Chicago, 1927.

Bobbie Leecan's Need-More Band, recorded 1927 in Camden, N.J., Bobbie Leecan, kazoo.

Memphis Jug Band, recorded 1928 in Memphis, Tenn., Ben Ramey, kazoo.

Jolly Joe and His Jug Band, Piedmont PLP 13160. 12″ LP, original recordings, ca. 1965 (performers probably white).

Joe Bussard, Bob Coltman, Jerry Marcum, kazoo.

The Jug Bands, RBF RF6. 12″ LP, original recordings by Sam Charters.

The Mobile Strugglers, recorded in Alabama, 1954, Ollie Crenshaw, on the kazoo.

Virgil Perkins, kazoo, recorded in Texas, 1955.

The Jug, Hook and Washboard Bands, Blues Classics 2. 12″ LP, reissues.

Dallas Jamboree Jug Band, recorded in Dallas, 1935, unknown kazoo player.

Ed Kelly's Washboard Band, recorded in North Carolina, 1937, performers' names unknown.

Memphis Jug Band, recorded in Memphis, Tenn., 1930, Ben Ramey, kazoo.

Walter Taylor's Washboard Band, recorded in Richmond, Ind., 1930, unknown kazoo player.

Jugs, Washboards and Kazoos,

RCA Victor LPV-540. 12″ LP, reissues.

Five Harmaniacs, recorded 1926, place unknown, Clyde Shugart, kazoo.

Index